The Fact-Packed ACTIVITY Book
INSECTS
AND OTHER TINY CREATURES

Contents

Senior Editors Kritika Gupta, Marie Greenwood
US Editor Jill Hamilton
US Senior Editor Shannon Beatty
Senior Art Editor Roohi Rais
Art Editors Nishtha Gupta, Aparajita Sen
Senior Jackets Art Editor Rashika Kachroo
DTP Designers Bimlesh Tiwary, Mohd Rizwan
Assistant Picture Research Administrator
Manpreet Kaur
Production Editor Jacqueline Street-Elkayam
Senior Production Controller Inderjit Bhullar
Managing Editors Monica Saigal, Gemma Farr
Managing Art Editors Ivy Sengupta,
Diane Peyton Jones
Delhi Creative Head Malavika Talukder
Art Director Mabel Chan

Consultant David Burnie
Educational Consultant Selina Wood

Material in this publication was previously published in:
Ultimate Factivity Collection Bugs (2015)

This American Edition, 2024
Published in the United States by DK Publishing,
a division of Penguin Random House LLC
1745 Broadway, 20th Floor, New York, NY 10019

Copyright © 2024 Dorling Kindersley Limited
24 25 26 27 28 10 9 8 7 6 5 4 3 2 1
001–340937–Nov/2024

All rights reserved.
Without limiting the rights under the copyright reserved above, no part of this publication may be reproduced, stored in or introduced into a retrieval system, or transmitted, in any form, or by any means (electronic, mechanical, photocopying, recording, or otherwise), without the prior written permission of the copyright owner. Published in Great Britain by Dorling Kindersley Limited

A catalog record for this book
is available from the Library of Congress.
ISBN: 978-0-5938-4375-8

DK books are available at special discounts when purchased in bulk for sales promotions, premiums, fund-raising, or educational use. For details, contact: DK Publishing Special Markets,
1745 Broadway, 20th Floor, New York, NY 10019
SpecialSales@dk.com

Printed and bound in China

www.dk.com

This book was made with Forest Stewardship Council™ certified paper—one small step in DK's commitment to a sustainable future. Learn more at
www.dk.com/uk/information/sustainability

Pages	Topic
4–5	How this book works
6–7	All about arthropods
8–9	What is an arthropod?
10–11	Ancient arthropods
12–13	What do I look like?
14–15	Arthropod families
16–17	Count my legs
18–19	Earth's most successful creatures
20–21	Butterfly or moth?
22–23	Lots of legs
24–25	Under the sea
26–27	Glow in the dark
28–29	Spot the difference
30–31	Learning about bugs
32–33	What do I do?
34–35	Adult and baby
36–37	Insect superpowers
38–39	Danger!
40–41	Helpful or harmful?
42–43	Bugs in your garden

44–45	Masters of disguise	80–81	A swarm of locusts
46–47	Eating bugs	82–83	Silent hunters
48–49	Let's fly	84–85	17-year cicadas
50–51	Seeing together	86–87	Buzz! Buzz!
52–53	The arthropod world	88–89	Helping bugs
54–55	Bugs & co. shopping	90–91	Design your own bug
56–57	Army of ants	92–93	Answers
58–59	What's an arachnid?	94–95	Glossary
60–61	Tarantula trouble	96	Acknowledgments
62–63	Beetle box		
64–65	Termite skyscraper		
66–67	Busy bees		
68–69	Living in the rainforest		
70–71	The unusual world of bugs		
72–73	Survival experts		
74–75	Wanted dead or alive		
76–77	Butterfly colors		
78–79	Weird and wonderful		

How this book works

Here is some information to help you find your way around this book, which is all about insects and other tiny creatures.

These boxes give fun facts about topics.

Activities
There are many exciting activities for you to do in this book. All you need is a pen or pencil, crayons, a little imagination, and a thirst for knowledge!

Look for this roundel on every spread. It tells you what the activity is.

MATCH each job to its description. Answers on pp. 92–93.

Instructions
All the instructions you'll need to complete an activity can be found on each page.

Answers
The answers to the questions are on pp. 92–93. Good luck!

Play and Learn
Read and Learn
Read and Create
Draw and Learn
Match and Learn
Look and Find
Test Your Knowledge

These are the different types of activity that you will find in the book:

1 **Play and Learn:** Follow the lines or join the dots to discover more about different animals.

2 **Read and Learn:** Read the information on the pages to learn more.

3 **Read and Create:** After reading the pages, use your coloring pens or pencils to color the pictures.

4 **Draw and Learn:** Get ready with your pencils to draw, learn, and have fun.

5 **Match and Learn:** Match the descriptions to the pictures.

6 **Look and Find:** Let's see how well you can spot the pictures in the book.

7 **Test Your Knowledge:** Test yourself by answering mind-boggling questions, and see if you've guessed correctly.

Introductions give you an overview of the topic that is being discussed on the pages.

Amazing activities will help you understand a specific topic better.

5

All about arthropods

When people say "bugs" they're usually thinking about insects. But insects are actually just one type of creature in a much larger group called arthropods.

1
2
3
4
5
6

FIND

where these pictures are on pp. 8–29. Check your answers on pp. 92–93.

Look and Find

7
8
9
10
11
12

What is an arthropod?

Arthropods are invertebrates, which means they don't have a backbone. They are the biggest group of animals on Earth, and they're also the most varied.

All insects are arthropods, but not all arthropods are insects!

Body structure
There are three things that all arthropods have in common—they all have a tough covering, jointed legs, and segmented bodies. Some arthropods, such as insects, also have wings.

Facts about...

Growing armor
An arthropod has a hard exoskeleton on the outside of its body, which **cannot grow**. So, it sheds its exoskeleton and makes a new one to grow bigger.

All arthropods have segmented bodies. This means their bodies are split into two or more parts.

Facts about... Habitats

Arthropods can be found **anywhere on Earth**. Many of them, such as crustaceans, live in aquatic habitats. Others, such as centipedes and many insects, live on land.

Test Your Knowledge

GUESS if the statements are true or false. Check your answers on pp. 92–93.

Arthropods have six or more jointed legs. In fact, the word arthropod means "jointed foot."

Arthropods have exoskeletons. Their bodies are hard on the outside and soft on the inside.

1. Lobsters, beetles, spiders, and butterflies are all arthropods.
2. Many species of arthropods are so tiny that they're actually too small to see.
3. An arthropod's jointed limbs make it flexible.
4. Most arthropods have seven body segments.
5. When an arthropod sheds its exoskeleton, it is molting.

Ancient arthropods

Arthropods have been on Earth longer than humans. Fossilized remains from about 359–299 million years ago suggest the existence of creatures similar to present-day insects, spiders, and crustaceans.

FIND the answers to the quiz questions. Check your answers on pp. 92–93.

Euphoberia
The euphoberia was a close prehistoric relative of the millipede. It lived on dry land and could measure up to 6 in (15 cm).

Fossils of this arthropod-like creature have been found in Europe and North America.

Meganeura
Similar to a dragonfly in appearance, this ancient arthropod had a wingspan of about 2.5 ft (70 cm). It had compound eyes with many lenses just like those of modern adult insects.

The wings of this insect were thin and made of a plasticlike, fibrous substance called chitin.

Facts about... Insect flight

In the prehistoric world, insects were the first animals to fly. They started flying at least **250 million years** before the first birds took to the air.

Stenodictya

This insect lived about 310 million years ago. Like most flying insects of the time, it had two pairs of wings. A herbivore, it used its mouthparts to suck sap from plants.

Archimylacris

Archimylacris lived 300 million years ago on the floor of early forests. An ancestor of the cockroach, mantis, and termite, it probably ate decaying plants and insects.

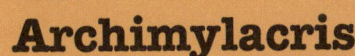
Archimylacris fossils can measure 0.8–3.5 in (2–9 cm) in length.

Gallio

This ancient scorpion shared several traits with its modern-day descendants. Much like today's scorpions, gallio had long, slender pincers and a long tail, which probably had a powerful sting.

Test Your Knowledge

Quiz

1. What was the wingspan of a Meganeura?
2. Euphoberia was an ancient relative of which modern-day arthropod?
3. How long ago did stenodictya live?
4. What did archimylacris probably eat?

What do I look like?

There are around a million different arthropod species, and they come in a variety of shapes and sizes. Do you think you can draw them accurately?

TIGER CENTIPEDE
- Its long body is made up of around 20 little segments.
- Each segment alternates between orange and black.
- It has two long antennae on its head.
- It has around 20 pairs of legs!

AMERICAN LOBSTER
- It is a bluish-green color.
- Its body is covered in a hard shell.
- The lobster has 10 legs, including its claws.
- Its claws are thicker and bigger than its legs.
- One claw is often bigger than the other.

RED-KNEED TARANTULA
- It has eight thick legs.
- Its body and legs are covered in small hairs.
- All its knees are an orangey-red color.
- The tarantula has a thick body split into two parts.

MONARCH BUTTERFLY
- Its body is long and slender.
- The butterfly has two pairs of wings.
- Its wings are bright orange with black lines and little white spots around the edges.
- The butterfly has two thin antennae on its head.

Facts about...

Groups

The million or so **arthropod species** are divided into four main groups: insects, arachnids, myriapods, and crustaceans.

DRAW the other half of the butterfly and then color it in.

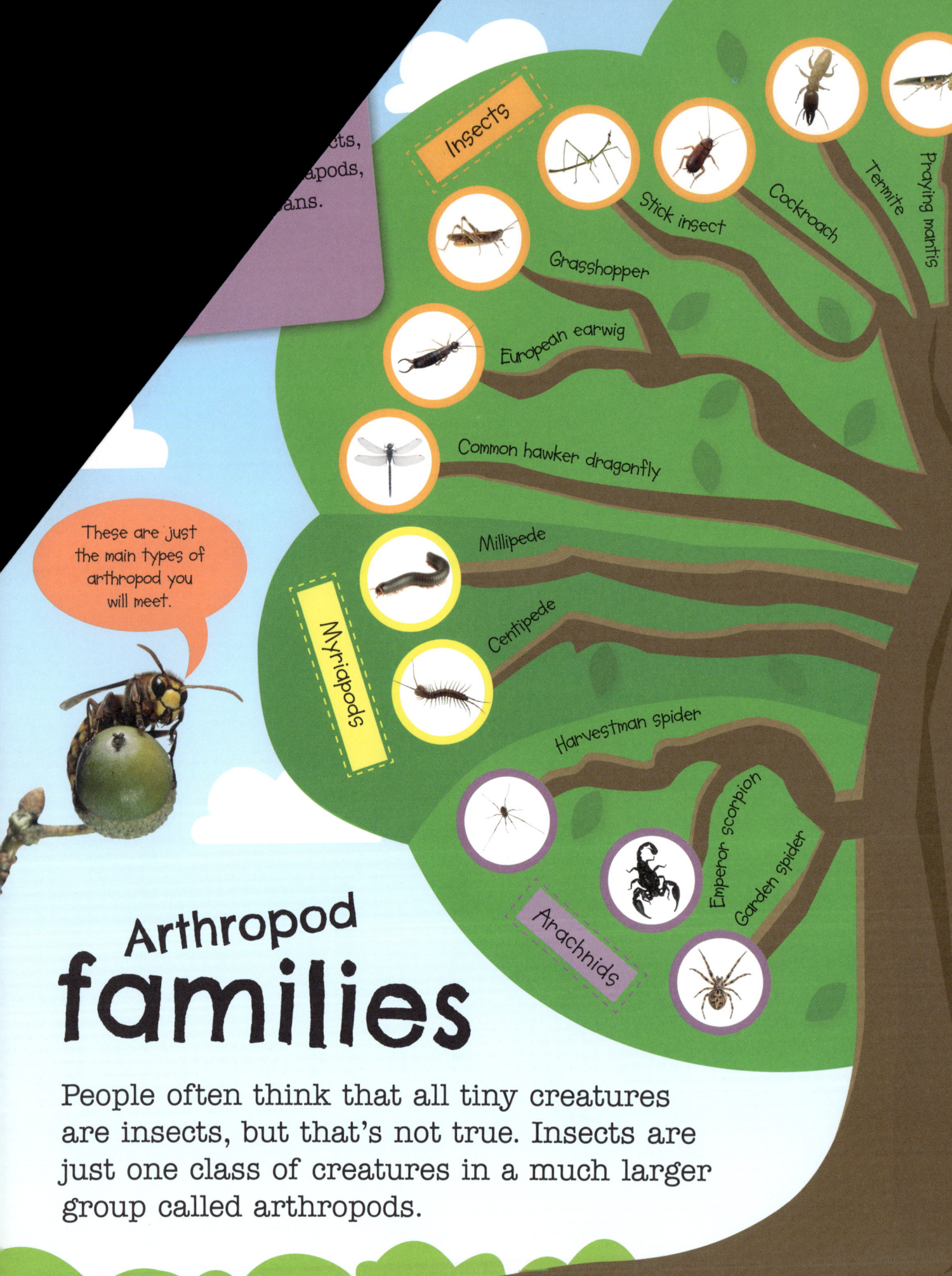

Arthropod families

People often think that all tiny creatures are insects, but that's not true. Insects are just one class of creatures in a much larger group called arthropods.

These are just the main types of arthropod you will meet.

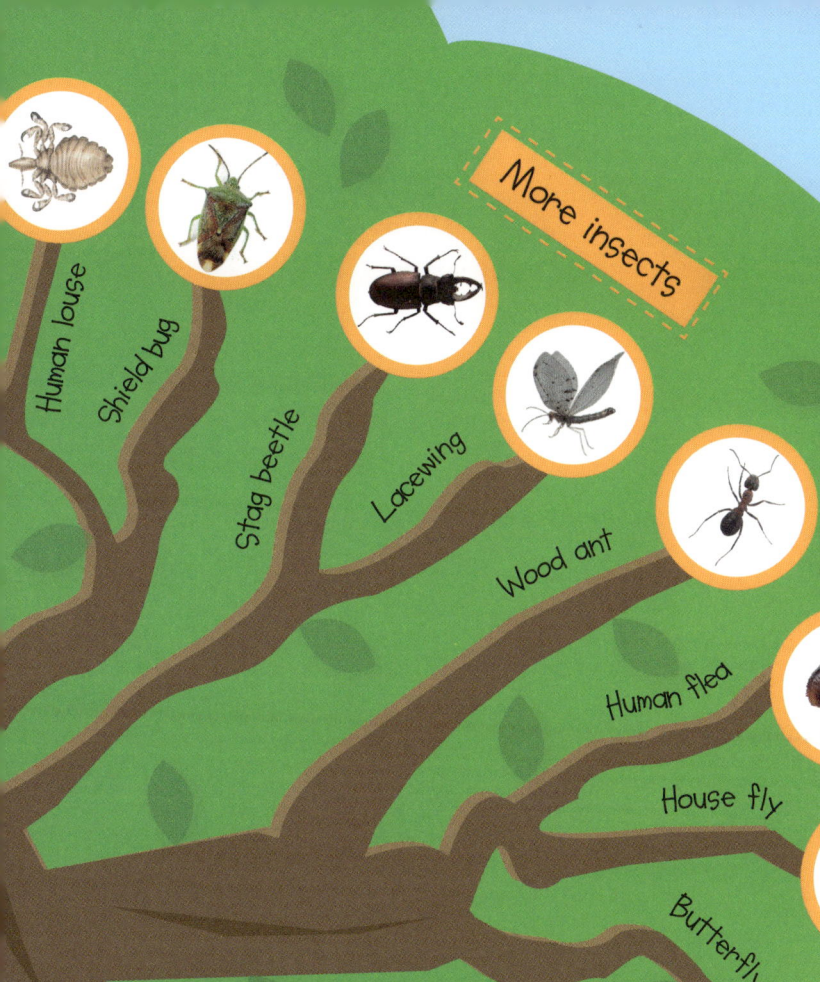

An arthropod's world
These are just some of the most common types of arthropods, but there can be thousands of different species of each. For example, there are more than 400,000 different species of beetles.

Read and Learn

READ about the different groups of arthropod.

Dragonflies first appeared 300 million years ago, long before the dinosaurs.

TRUE OR FALSE? ARTHROPOD SPECIES ARE DIVIDED INTO FOUR MAIN GROUPS.

Facts about...

The first arthropods
By studying **fossils**, experts know that arthropods have been around for almost **half a billion years**. And they all evolved from worms!

15

Count my legs

It can be hard to tell if a creature is an insect or another type of arthropod. There are a few ways to tell them apart, but one of the easiest ways is to look at its legs.

6 Insect: If a creature has six legs it's probably an insect. Most insects have a body that is divided into three sections: a head, a thorax (chest), and an abdomen (belly).

8 Arachnid: Most people know spiders and scorpions, but ticks and mites are arachnids too. All adult arachnids have eight legs, and none have wings.

10 Crustacean: While some crustaceans live on land, most of them live in water. They usually have 10 legs but some can have more.

30+ Myriapod: If a creature has lots of legs, it's probably a centipede or millipede. These have long bodies made up of lots of segments.

Spider pedipalps (which are for feeling or holding) aren't legs.

1. Myriapod or arachnid?

COUNT the legs of the creatures, then work out which type they are. Answers on pp. 92–93.

2. Insect or crustacean?

Earth's most successful creatures

It might seem like humans rule the world, but arthropods have been around a lot longer, and there are many more of them than any other type of creature on Earth.

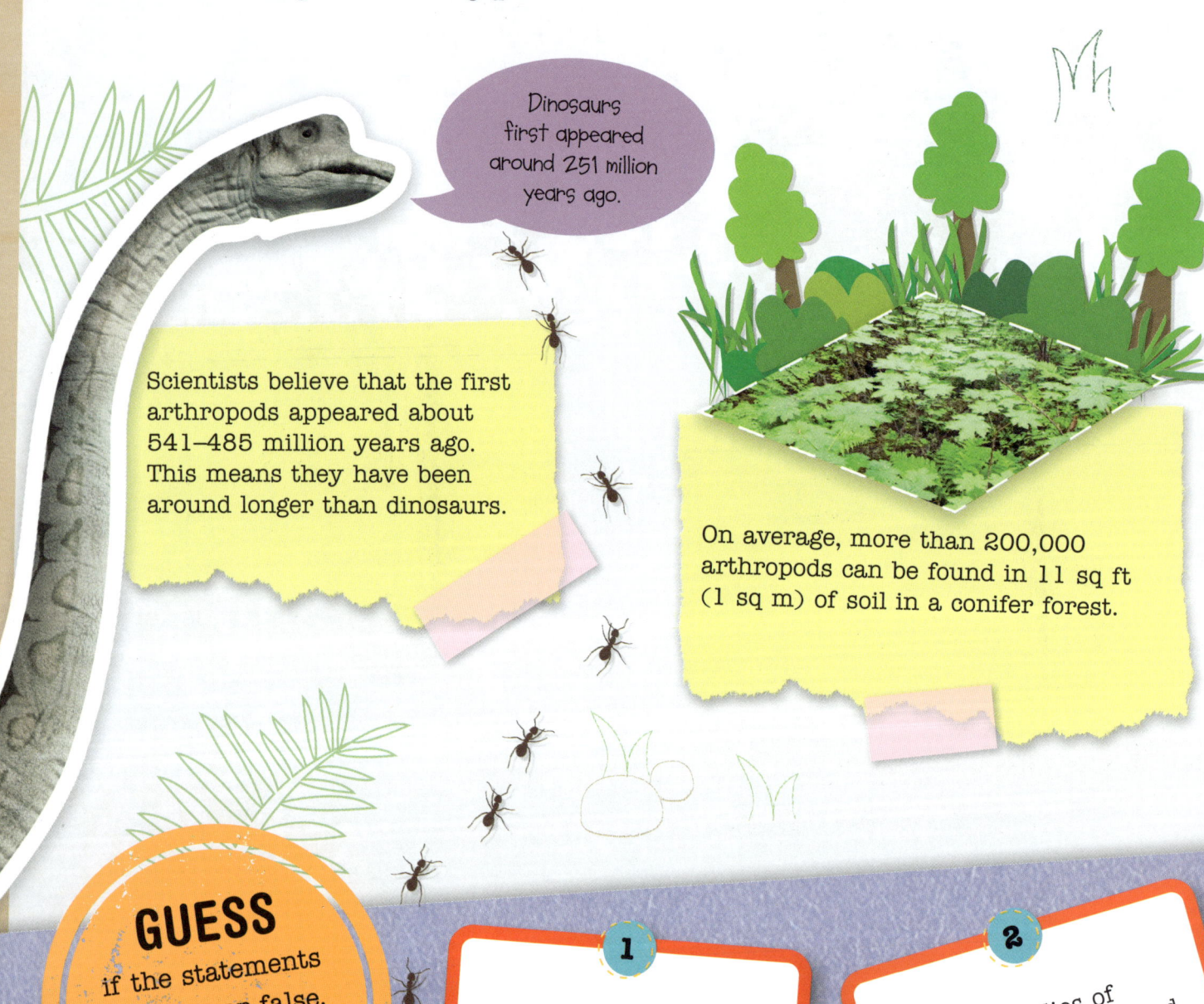

Dinosaurs first appeared around 251 million years ago.

Scientists believe that the first arthropods appeared about 541–485 million years ago. This means they have been around longer than dinosaurs.

On average, more than 200,000 arthropods can be found in 11 sq ft (1 sq m) of soil in a conifer forest.

GUESS if the statements are true or false. Check your answers on pp. 92–93.

1 There are 80 different kinds of arthropod species in the world.

2 The bodies of arthropods are divided into segments.

There are more than 8 billion humans on Earth and there are more than 1 billion insects alive for every human.

It's thought that there are about 8.7 living species on Earth and more than 85 percent of them are arthropods.

Test Your Knowledge

There are more than 900,000 known species of insects, making them the largest group of arthropods.

Facts about... Ecosystem

Arthropods have an **important role** in different ecosystems. Some arthropods, such as bees, help in **pollination**, while others, such as centipedes, make **nutrients for the soil** by breaking down dead plants and animals.

3 All insects are harmful to humans and other animals.

4 Butterflies and crabs are both arthropods.

5 Many species of arthropods go through a metamorphosis.

Butterfly

The Queen Alexandra's birdwing is the largest butterfly in the world. The male has a wingspan of 8 in (20 cm) and the female is even larger!

READ
about butterflies and moths, and find out some fun facts about them.

Butterflies can only fly when their bodies are warm enough, so they **fly in the day or at dusk**—not night-time.

Most butterflies have long, **thin antennae** with rounded tips at the end.

Butterflies
These pretty insects are best known for their bright colors and symmetrical wing patterns. Did you know they're related to moths?

Almost all butterflies have thin and **smooth bodies**.

When resting, most butterflies position their **wings** so that they're **upright and together**.

A butterfly's **chrysalis** has a hard shell and usually hangs from a leaf.

Butterflies and moths belong to the same group of insects, and in many ways they're very similar. However, there are a few simple ways to tell them apart.

TRUE OR FALSE?
THE QUEEN ALEXANDRA'S BIRDWING IS THE LARGEST MOTH IN THE WORLD.

or Moth?

With a wingspan of up to 30 cm (12 in), the Atlas moth is one of the biggest in the world.

Moths
Most people probably think of moths as the dull-looking creatures that ruin our clothes, but they can also come in lots of beautiful colors as well.

Read and Learn

Some moths fly during the day, but most **fly at night**. They vibrate their flight muscles to warm up.

Moth **antennae** are a bit like brushes. They use them to sense their way at night.

Moth **bodies** are **thicker** than those of butterflies, and are covered with fuzz to keep them warm.

A moth will usually rest with its **wings open and flat**.

Instead of a chrysalis, most moth caterpillars spin a **cocoon** on or under the ground.

A magnified view of a butterfly wing.

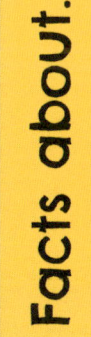

Facts about... Scaly wings
Butterfly and moth wings look soft, but they are made of lots of hard **chitin** scales—a material very similar to keratin, which is what our fingernails are made of.

Lots of legs

Millipedes and centipedes belong to a group of arthropods called myriapods. They may look like insects at first, but there's one key difference—the number of legs they have!

A millipede has two pairs of legs on each segment.

Millipede
The Latin word "mille" means thousand, but most millipedes have around 60 legs (although some have 750, and one has more than 1,000!).

Feeds on rotting plants

Will sink in water ↓

Centipede
A lot of people think all centipedes have 100 legs, but the number actually ranges from about 20 to 300.

Feeds on small animals

Will float in water ↑

Facts about...

Fossils
Myriapods are one of the **oldest types** of arthropods—a centipede fossil has been found that dates back almost 430 million years.

Centipedes can be venomous.

Venomous centipedes can inject their prey with a paralyzing venom.

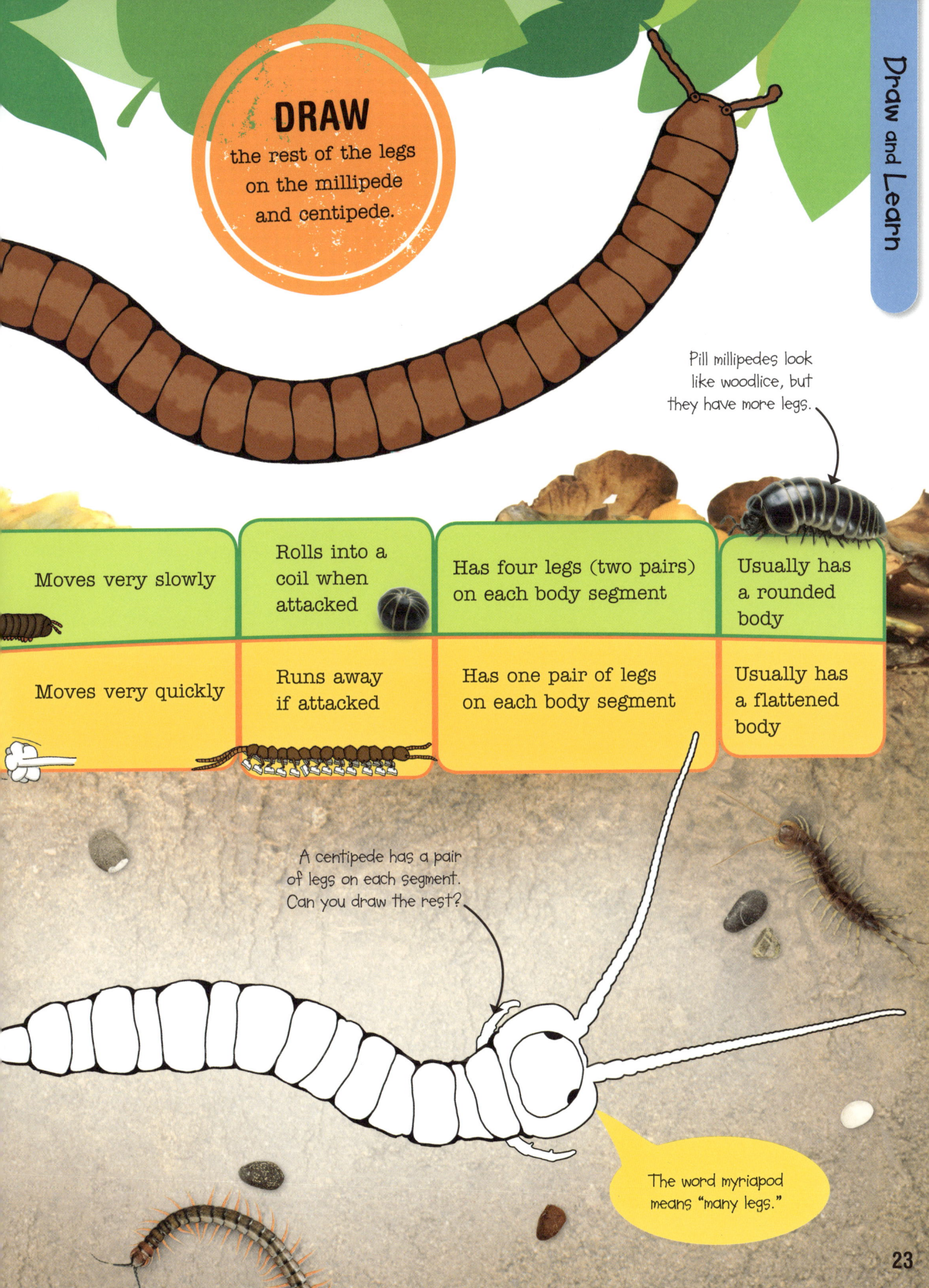

Under the sea

Crabs can walk on land, but almost all crustaceans live in water. Woodlice are one of the few species that live on land.

1 European lobster
A lobster has a hard, armorlike outer covering to protect its soft body. It uses its antennae to feel its way around the seabed, and has claws to catch and cut food.

2 Dungeness crab
Found along the Pacific coast, it is also known as the common crab. The top of its shell is reddish-brown, while its legs are yellowish.

3 Common prawn
The common prawn has translucent skin and usually lives in a group. It can be found in rock cracks and under stones at a depth of up to 131 ft (40 m).

MATCH each crustacean to its description. Check your answers on pp. 92–93.

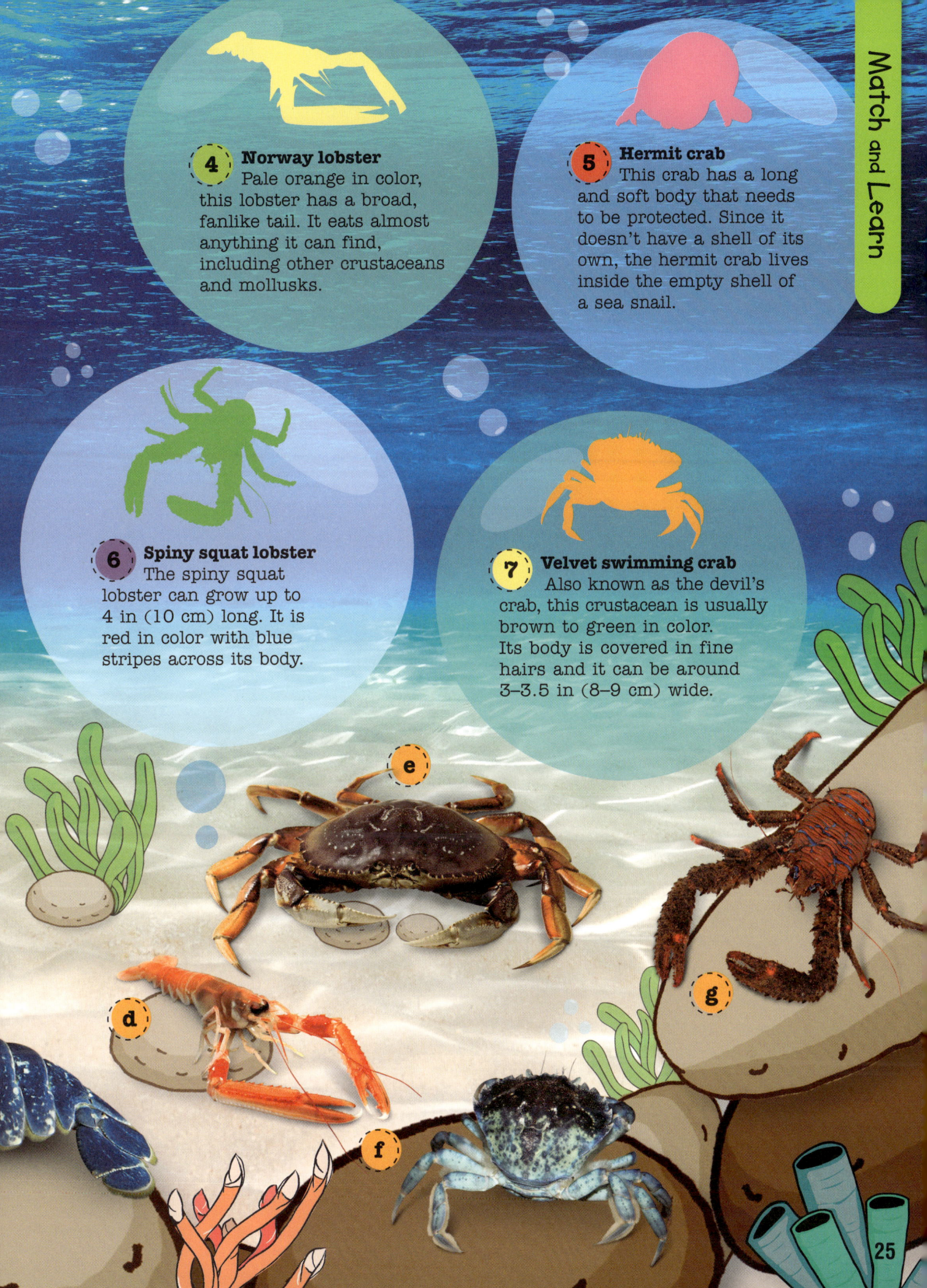

Glow in the dark

Some types of insects make their own light, enabling them to glow in the dark. These insects are called bioluminescent. They use this light to communicate with one another, to find food, and even to warn off predators.

Railroad worm
Glowing spots run down both sides of a railroad worm's body. The spots look similar to lit train windows, which gives the railroad worm its name.

CONNECT the dots to see what a railroad worm looks like.

Draw and Learn

Click beetle
Click beetles don't usually look that flashy during daytime, but after dark their eyespots and abdomen begin to glow. The glow can be seen from far away.

Motyxia
The only millipedes known to be bioluminescent are called motyxia. These insects are found only in a small region of the Sierra Nevada mountain range in California, US.

Fireflies
Fireflies flash their light to communicate with each other or find mates. Their blinking also warns off predators. Different firefly species have different blinking patterns.

Glow-worm
Glow-worms are not actually worms but beetles. They use their light to communicate and attract a mate. The female glow-worms are wingless, while males can fly.

Facts about...

Light show
Flashes from fireflies can be **yellow, green, or orange**. Even the eggs and babies of fireflies glow to warn predators and send a message that they don't taste very nice.

Spot the difference

Look at the big and small **insects** in your garden! All kinds of bugs, such as slugs, ladybugs, bees, and butterflies, can be found scuttling or fluttering around in backyards.

SPOT eight differences between the two pictures.

Butterflies can be seen fluttering around flowers in the garden.

Facts about... Garden bugs

Gardens have lots of **plants** that provide food and shelter to bugs. Some bugs, such as aphids, damage plants. Others, such as earthworms, are good for the soil.

Look and Find

29

Learning about bugs

Our planet has many different kinds of arthropods. While some are harmful, others are useful. Some bugs, including shrimp and crickets, can even be eaten by humans.

FIND

where these pictures are on pp. 32–51. Check your answers on pp. 92–93.

Look and Find

What do I do?

There are far more arthropods on Earth than any other type of animal, so there are lots of different jobs that involve studying, harvesting, and managing them.

Pest exterminator

Conservationist

Entomologist

Forensic entomologist

Beekeeper

1 I'm called to crime scenes to **study** flies and maggots for important clues. I am a...

MATCH each job to its description. Answers on pp.92–93.

2 I help to **get rid of** annoying pests that cause all sorts of problems for people. I am a...

3 I work to **conserve** and **protect wildlife** and the environment. I am a...

4 I help **manage colonies of bees** so that I can collect their delicious honey. I am a...

5 It's my job to **study** insect species to learn more about them. I am an...

Match and Learn

33

Yellow swallowtail
The yellow swallowtail caterpillar has a striped body with orange spots.

Adult and baby

Insects and other arthropods don't grow up in the same way as most other creatures do. Instead of just getting bigger they can completely change size, color, and shape.

Mayfly
Mayfly babies (nymphs) are brown in color and are good swimmers.

FOLLOW the lines to find each insect's baby.

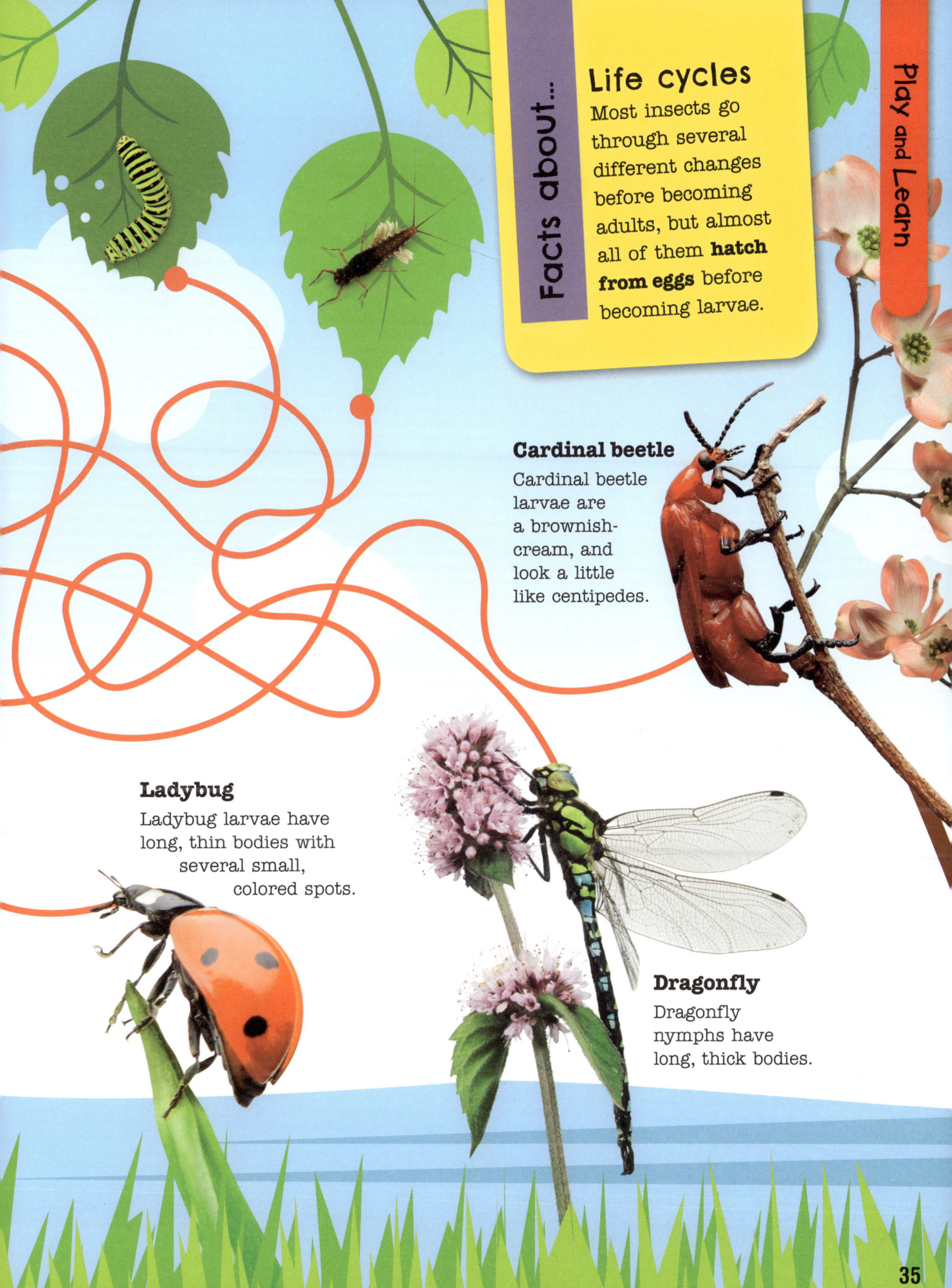

Life cycles

Facts about...

Most insects go through several different changes before becoming adults, but almost all of them **hatch from eggs** before becoming larvae.

Play and Learn

Cardinal beetle
Cardinal beetle larvae are a brownish-cream, and look a little like centipedes.

Ladybug
Ladybug larvae have long, thin bodies with several small, colored spots.

Dragonfly
Dragonfly nymphs have long, thick bodies.

Insect superpowers

Insects may be small, but that doesn't mean they're not special. Because of the way the laws of physics work on tiny things, it can seem like they have superpowers.

GUESS if the statements are true or false. Check your answers on pp. 92–93.

1 The rhinoceros beetle can lift up to 850 times its own body weight.

850 times a human's weight would be as much as a tank!

I can walk up walls with ease! Can you?

2 Some species of flies are totally invisible, and can only be seen with special glasses.

Facts about... Forces

Insects don't really have superpowers. It just seems like they do because **forces that involve weight**, such as jumping and lifting, are much easier at such tiny sizes.

Test Your Knowledge

3 If the cat flea was the size of a human it would be able to jump as high as Mt. Everest.

4 Moths are so light, they can fly as fast as jumbo jets.

5 Certain ants are so strong they can drag objects 1,500 times as heavy as them.

6 Pond skaters can walk on water without sinking.

Danger!

Here are several ways that arthropods can cause harm.

CONNECT the dots to reveal the rest of the picture, then color it in.

Spiky surprise

The **postman caterpillar** has two means of defense. Not only is it poisonous but its soft body is covered in sharp, protective spikes.

Tail barb

Scorpions, like the **desert scorpion**, have barbed tails that can be used to paralyze or sometimes kill their enemies and prey.

Deadly bite

Not all spiders have a deadly bite, but the **black widow** is so venomous, it can kill small animals and sometimes even people.

A nasty sting

Like some bees, **wasps** can use their stingers to hurt their enemies. Unlike bees, though, wasps can sting repeatedly and survive.

They may be small, but that doesn't mean they're harmless. Many arthropods have developed deadly ways of attacking prey or fighting back against predators.

Facts about... Chemical spray

The bombardier beetle stores the chemicals inside **two separate parts** of its body. When attacked, it mixes them, causing them to react and explode.

Draw and Learn

A surprising spray

The bombardier beetle has an unusual way of defending itself. It fends off predators by spraying boiling chemicals at them. Smaller predators can be blinded or even killed by it.

39

Helpful or harmful?

Most insects are harmless to humans, and play a vital part in nature by providing food for other creatures and by recycling waste, but others are pests that cause big problems.

DRAW a happy face for helpful, sad face for harmful, or both if you think it's needed. Answers on pp. 92–93.

1. **Aphids** eat their way through a lot of plants and crops, so are a nuisance to gardeners and farmers.

2. **Fruit flies** can spread germs, but scientists have studied and used them in genetics experiments.

Here's a hint for you.

3. **Fleas** can infest dogs, cats, and humans. They suck blood for food and it causes intense itching and pain.

Many insects are helpful because they control other insect populations.

A world without insects

A world without insects would definitely make picnics nicer, but the food chain would collapse and we'd be buried in dead plants and animals!

4. Bees pollinate plants, which helps us to grow food, but their sting can be deadly to people with allergies.

5. Dung beetles feed on decaying material and the dung of other creatures. This cleans up waste and keeps the soil healthy.

6. Maggots feed on dead flesh and doctors sometimes use them to clean wounds, but they breed in large numbers and can cause infestations.

7. Termites eat wood, which causes problems in houses and other buildings. But they also help recycle dead and decaying trees.

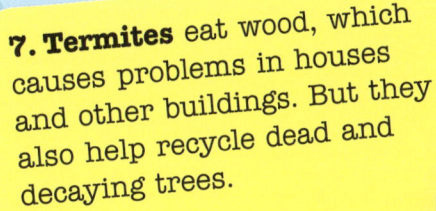

Maggots are the larvae of flies.

8. Female mosquitoes carry and spread many deadly diseases, such as malaria and dengue fever.

bzzzz bzzzz bzzzz

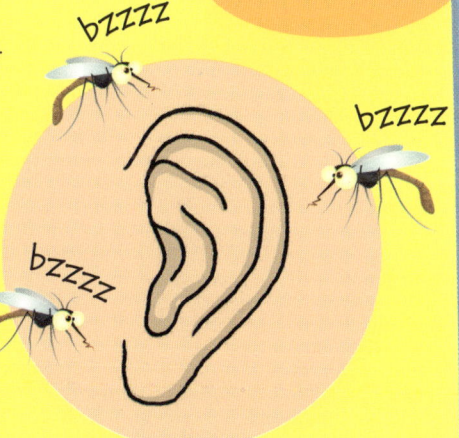

The food chain

Facts about...

Every insect, no matter how tiny or insignificant it might seem, has an effect on the food chain. So **all insects are important**, even if they're also harmful.

Draw and Learn

Bugs in your garden

READ
about the different bugs you might find in a garden.

An entire world of bugs can be found in your garden. Here, insects can find everything they need to survive, including food and shelter.

Social wasps and honeybees
While they may look similar from a distance, these bugs are very different from each other up close. Social wasps are yellow-and-black with long bodies, while honeybees are more orange and have rounder bodies.

Facts about... Plant eaters
There are many plant-eating insects in the garden. They **munch on** different parts of a plant, including new green shoots, leaves, and even flower nectar.

Earthworms
Commonly found in gardens, earthworms are actually invertebrates, which means they don't have a backbone. They spend most of their lives underground, using their soft, thin bodies to tunnel through the soil.

Read and Learn

Facts about...

Scavengers
Scavengers are insects that don't eat living plants or animals but feed on **almost anything else**. They eat rotting plants, the dead bodies of other animals, garbage, and even our food.

Butterflies and moths
Butterflies and moths are often found near garden flowers. These insects have two pairs of broad wings, which can have attractive patterns on them.

Beetles
Beetles usually have a hard case around their wings for protection. They can be of different shapes and vary in size.

Centipedes and millipedes
Mostly found on or in the soil, these insects have segmented bodies. While millipedes are herbivores and usually eat roots and leaves, centipedes are carnivores that eat other insects.

TRUE OR FALSE?
SCAVENGER INSECTS EAT PLANTS AND OTHER SMALLER INSECTS.

Masters of disguise

Insects and other arthropods have adapted to be able to blend into their surroundings and stay hidden. They do this to hide from predators or to surprise their prey.

Forest leaf grasshopper
This grasshopper looks so much like a leaf that it's almost impossible to tell the difference even when you know it's there!

Thorn bug
They may look like thorns on a branch, but they're actually bugs (or treehoppers). If you look closely you can see their legs.

Cracker butterfly
It's more common in moths, but butterflies such as the cracker butterfly can look like the bark of a tree while perched.

Stick caterpillar
The color and markings of this caterpillar make it look like a branch or twig. It's very hard for a predator to spot.

When **leaf insects** move, their bodies rock back and forth. This makes them look just like a leaf being blown in the wind.

Is that a leaf? What a good disguise!

Facts about... Camouflage
Blending in like this is called camouflage. It's not just animals that do this. **Army uniforms** are made to be camouflaged so that soldiers are harder to spot.

Test Your Knowledge

Quiz

1. Why do insects blend into their surroundings and stay hidden?

2. Which grasshopper looks like a leaf?

3. What is another name for thorn bugs?

4. Which butterfly can look like the bark of a tree?

FIND the answers to the quiz questions. Check your answers on pp. 92–93.

Can you spot the hiding mantis?

This shield bug would be hard to spot among leaves.

A hidden threat

While most bugs blend in to protect themselves, others, such as mantises, do it to remain hidden so they can ambush prey.

Eating bugs

Arthropods are an important source of food. In fact, up to 80 percent of the world's population eat them regularly.

TRUE OR FALSE?
THE WORD FOR HUMANS EATING INSECTS IS "ENTOMOPHAGY."

COUNT each type of arthropod on the plate below. Answers on pp. 92–93.

Facts about... Edible arthropods

Not all arthropods are edible—lots of them are poisonous. It's thought that there are roughly **2,000** different species that are eaten by humans.

Dinner time

Crustaceans, such as lobsters and crabs, are arthropods that many people eat. Here are a few other arthropods that can be eaten.

Menu

Look and Find

Shrimp are cooked in a variety of ways all over the world.

Silkworm pupae are very popular in Japan and other parts of Asia.

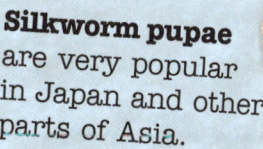

Water bugs are usually deep-fried and covered with salt.

Mealworms are eaten as healthy and crunchy snacks.

Scorpions are cooked on skewers in Thailand and China.

Crickets are a very nutritious snack that are usually toasted.

Let's fly

People like to call bugs creepy-crawlies, but a surprisingly large number of them can take to the air and soar through the sky!

Indian cicada

Cockchafer beetle

Hoverfly

Green-eyed dragonfly

Longwing butterfly

Lacewing

Seeing together

Many arthropods have eyes that are made up of lots of tiny lenses. Each of these lenses sends a different image to its brain. This is called compound eyesight.

1

3

Facts about... Compound eyes

Having big compound eyes enables insects to look in almost **all directions**. Their eyes can also sense movement, which helps them avoid attackers.

Match and Learn

MATCH the picture of each insect to its description.

2

4

a Spider
Most spiders have eight eyes but they don't have very good eyesight. Instead, they use their sense of touch to find their way around.

b Horsefly
When light is reflected from the shiny lenses in a horsefly's eye, it can create a very pretty rainbow pattern.

c Dragonfly
The eyes of dragonflies are bigger than the rest of their heads. They can spot prey in all directions while flying through the air.

d Stalk-eyed fly
The stalk-eyed fly's eyes are attached to the ends of long, narrow stalks that are almost the same length as its body.

The arthropod world

Insects and other arthropods experience and interact with the world in a very different way from us. Turn the pages to discover just how different they really are.

1
2
3
4
5
6

Bugs & co. shopping

How may I help you?

FOLLOW the lines to discover what each arthropod gives us.

OPEN

Pollination
By far the most important thing that insects do for us is pollinating plants. Without them doing this, we wouldn't be able to grow crops for food. Bats and birds pollinate as well, but not as much as insects.

1. No-see-um
2. Horseshoe crab
3. Silkworm
4. Honeybee
5. Cochineal beetle

Cochineal beetles live on cacti.

Arthropods do a lot of work for the planet, but they're also useful to humans in other ways. This includes scientific research or helping us create various products.

Play and Learn

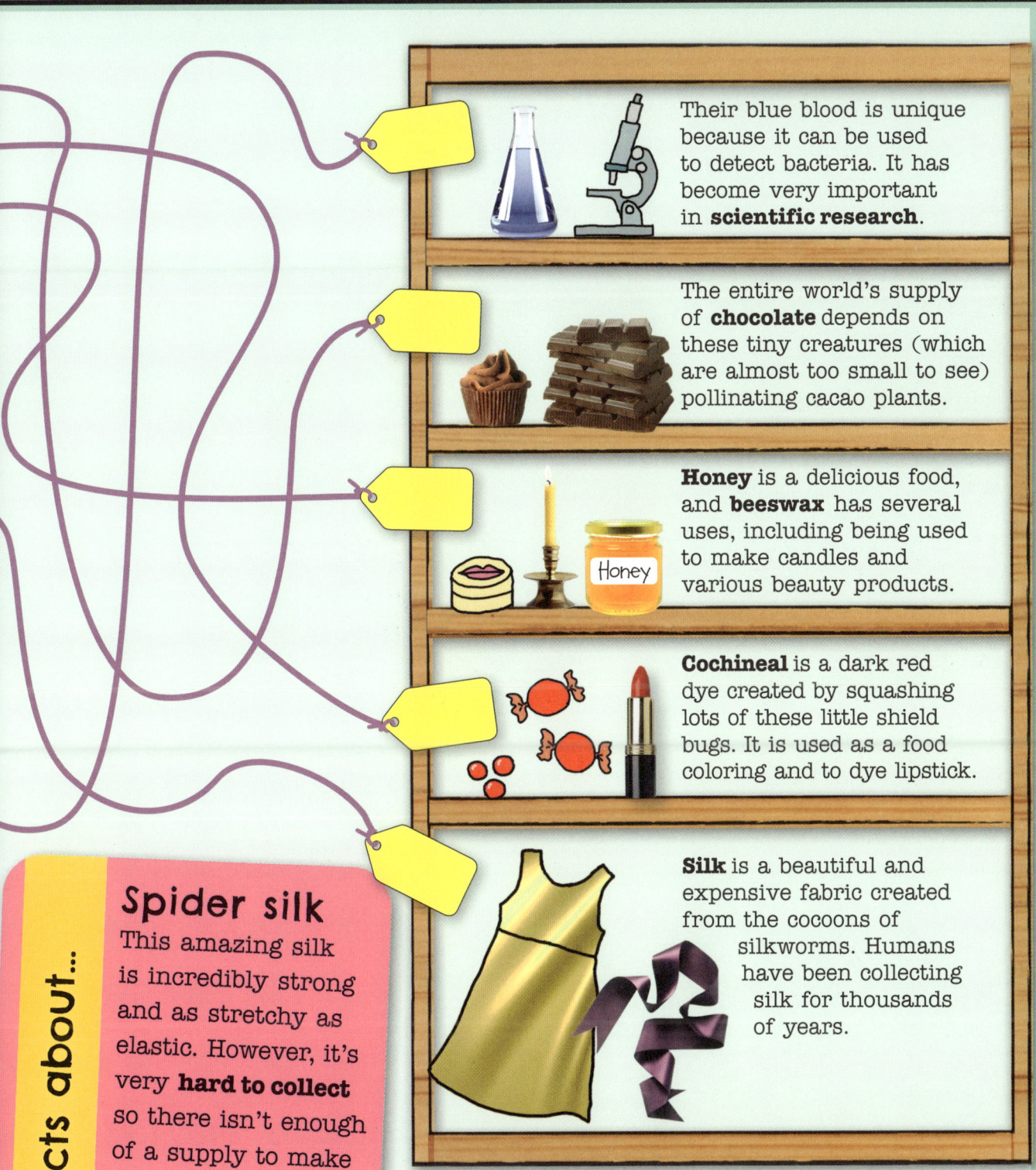

Their blue blood is unique because it can be used to detect bacteria. It has become very important in **scientific research**.

The entire world's supply of **chocolate** depends on these tiny creatures (which are almost too small to see) pollinating cacao plants.

Honey is a delicious food, and **beeswax** has several uses, including being used to make candles and various beauty products.

Cochineal is a dark red dye created by squashing lots of these little shield bugs. It is used as a food coloring and to dye lipstick.

Silk is a beautiful and expensive fabric created from the cocoons of silkworms. Humans have been collecting silk for thousands of years.

Facts about...

Spider silk

This amazing silk is incredibly strong and as stretchy as elastic. However, it's very **hard to collect** so there isn't enough of a supply to make many things with it.

55

Army of ants

Ants might look tiny and unimportant, but they're impressive insects that live in complex societies. In fact, ants are some of the most successful animals on Earth.

Facts about...

Teamwork
Ant colonies can be home for **thousands** of ants, so cooperation is very important. Ants build together, work together, and they raise their young together.

- Antennae
- Mandibles
- Eyes
- Head
- Thorax
- Abdomen
- Jointed leg

Ant biology
There are more than 12,000 species of ants, and they range in size from about 0.08 in (2 mm) to 1 in (2.5 cm) long. However, the body shape of most species is quite similar.

1 Ants have been around for almost 250 million years.

2 Ants are closely related to wasps and bees.

3 Fire ants all attack at the same time so they can cause more damage.

Ants vs humans

	Ants		Humans
🐜	There are around 20,000,000,000,000,000 (20 quadrillion) ants on Earth.	👤	There are around 8,000,000,000 (8 billion) humans on Earth.
🐜	Certain species of ants can lift more than 50 times their body weight.	👤	Most humans can't lift their own body weight.
🐜	Ants have existed for more than 100 million years.	👤	Humans have existed for about 3 million years.
🐜	Ant society relies on ants performing a range of different jobs.	👤	Human society does too.
🐜	Almost all the ants in a colony are female.	👤	About half of humans are female.

Test Your Knowledge

While most ants look quite similar, different species have different traits. This ant has **large mandibles** to help it attack and defend.

GUESS if the statements are true or false. Check your answers on pp. 92–93.

4 A species of ant found in Japan can grow to be 3 ft (1 m) long.

5 The only continent where ants aren't found is Antarctica.

6 The bullet ant has one of the most painful bites or stings of any insect.

Harvestmen look like spiders but can't spin webs. They also don't have fangs like spiders do.

Whip scorpions have eight legs. They use six legs for walking sideways and two long front legs (whips) to feel for their prey.

I can hang in the air from one strand of my spider silk.

Many species of spider, such as the **wasp spider**, trap prey in their webs and inject them with a paralyzing venom.

Scorpions use their powerful pincers (called pedipalps) to catch prey and then sting them with their deadly tail barb.

What's an arachnid?

They may look like insects, but arachnids are totally different creatures. There are lots of types, but the one thing they have in common is that they all have eight legs.

Not all spiders spin webs, but those that do create many different patterns.

Some spiders, such as this **Guyana pinktoe tarantula**, don't catch their prey using webs. Instead they lie in wait ready to ambush their victims.

Mites and ticks are usually too small to see, but they're everywhere. A person's bed might contain millions!

Actual size of a redlegged earth mite.

FIND the answers to the quiz questions. Answers on pp. 92–93.

Quiz

1 What do scorpions use to catch and sting prey?
- a. Fangs
- b. Pincers
- c. Whips
- d. Webs

2 How strong is spider silk?
- a. Five times stronger than a piece of steel
- b. Four times stronger than wool
- c. Twice as strong as cotton
- d. As strong as wood

3 Which arachnids are usually too small to see?
- a. Harvestmen
- b. Scorpions
- c. Mites and ticks
- d. Spiders

4 How do wasp spiders trap their prey?
- a. In their webs
- b. Ambush them
- c. Walk sideways
- d. Sting them

Test Your Knowledge

Facts about...

Spider silk
The webs that spiders spin are made of something called spider silk, which is five times **stronger than a piece of steel** that is the same thickness.

Tarantula trouble

Tarantulas are large spiders with hairy bodies and legs. They move slowly on their eight legs but are skilled hunters. Tarantulas mainly feed on insects but may also attack bigger animals, such as mice, frogs, and toads.

Goliath birdeater
The world's largest spider, the Goliath birdeater's body can measure around 4.5 in (12 cm). It usually eats insects but can grow large enough to feed on birds, lizards, and mice.

Cobalt blue
The cobalt blue tarantula comes from the rainforests of Thailand and Myanmar. It spends most of its time in its burrow, and only comes out to hunt and eat. The shimmering blue color of its legs makes this spider easy to identify.

Gooty sapphire
Also known as the "peacock tarantula" because of its colors, the gooty sapphire spider lives in the deciduous forests of Andhra Pradesh in India.

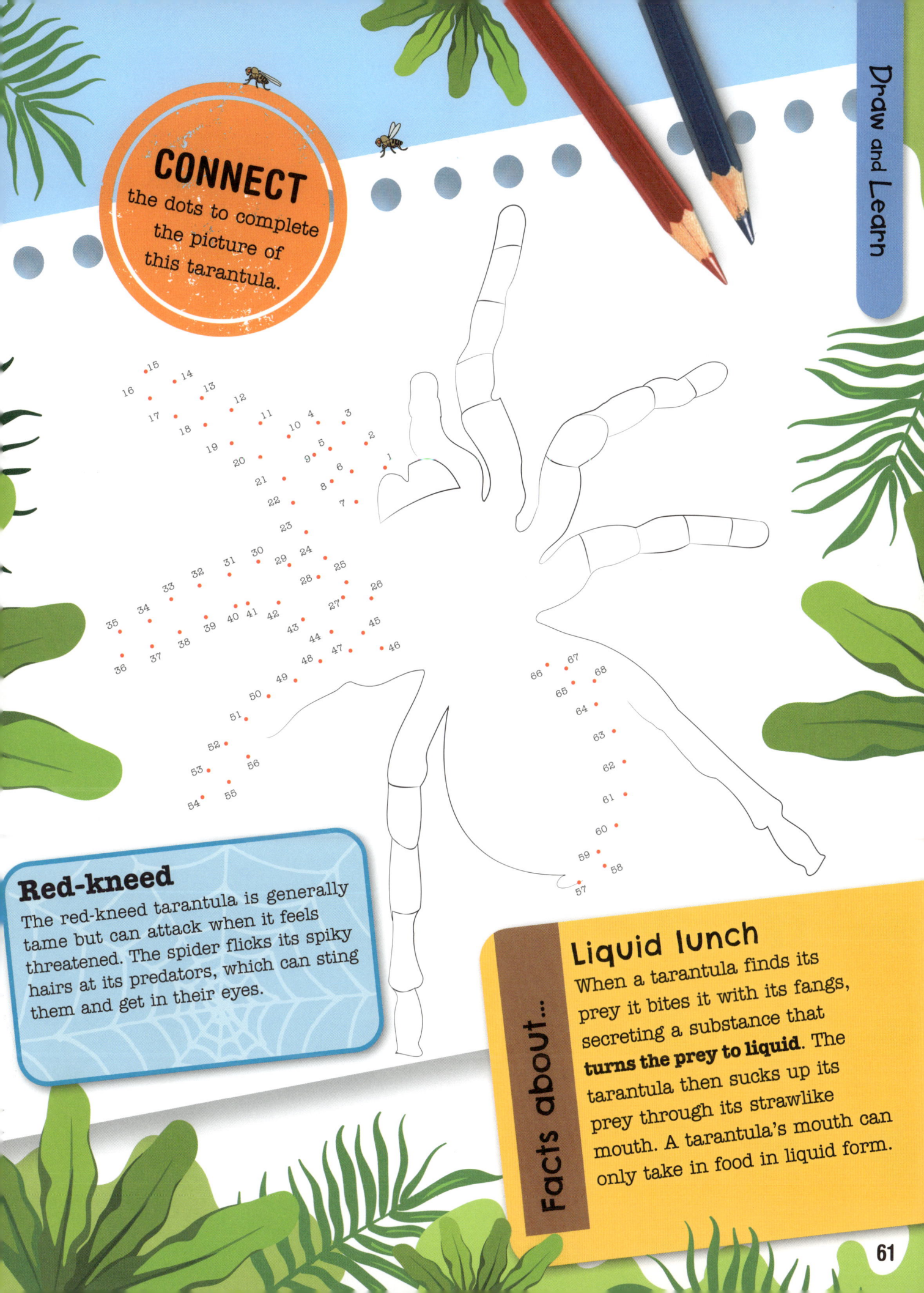

CONNECT
the dots to complete the picture of this tarantula.

Red-kneed
The red-kneed tarantula is generally tame but can attack when it feels threatened. The spider flicks its spiky hairs at its predators, which can sting them and get in their eyes.

Facts about...

Liquid lunch
When a tarantula finds its prey it bites it with its fangs, secreting a substance that **turns the prey to liquid**. The tarantula then sucks up its prey through its strawlike mouth. A tarantula's mouth can only take in food in liquid form.

Beetle box

Of all the insect species in the world, a third of them are beetles. They're also some of Earth's most diverse creatures, and come in many different sizes, shapes, and colors.

TRUE OR FALSE? THERE ARE AN ESTIMATED 400,000 DIFFERENT SPECIES OF BEETLE IN THE WORLD.

READ about the different kinds of beetle.

The **hercules beetle** belongs to the rhinoceros beetle family, and can lift up to 850 times its own body weight.

The heaviest beetle in the world, the **goliath beetle** can weigh as much as 3½ oz (100 g) and grow to be 6 in (15 cm) long.

Famous for their antennae that can be longer than their bodies, there are more than 30,000 species of **longhorn beetle**.

The **stag beetle** is one of the best-known species of beetle in the world. Males have powerful jaws to fight their rivals.

Unlike most beetles, the **click beetle** can move its head and front pair of legs separately from the rest of its body.

Facts about... Wings

Most beetles have two pairs of wings, one for flying, and a **second hardened pair** to protect the ones they fly with. These hard wings are called elytra.

Named for its thick hind legs that look like a frog's, the **jeweled frog beetle** can be found in tropical forests.

The rare **jewel scarab beetle**, which is usually a gold or silver in color, is mostly found in parts of Central and South America.

The male **giraffe weevil** has a very long neck, which can be up to three times as long as the female's.

Weevils, like this **jewel weevil**, are the largest family in the animal world. They have long snouts called "rostrums."

The ancient Egyptians believed the **scarab beetle** symbolized the cycle of life and rebirth. It can be seen in lots of ancient art.

The **Namibian fog-basking darkling beetle** survives by collecting moisture from fog that rolls in from the coast.

The **violin beetle** has a flat body so it can fit between the layers of fungi that grow on the trees where it lives.

This **African jewel beetle** possibly gathers pollen on its back so predators can't see it while it sits on flowers.

A chemical reaction allows **fireflies** to emit a glowing light from their abdomen. They do this to communicate.

Sometimes called a June bug, the **green June beetle** has dull green wings and a shiny green underside.

The colorful **lily leaf beetle** feeds on lily plants, and is considered a pest by gardeners.

Most commonly red, **ladybugs** can also be yellow, orange, or black. The number of spots they have varies.

Tortoise beetles have oval-shaped bodies, and are best known for their interesting dome-shaped elytra.

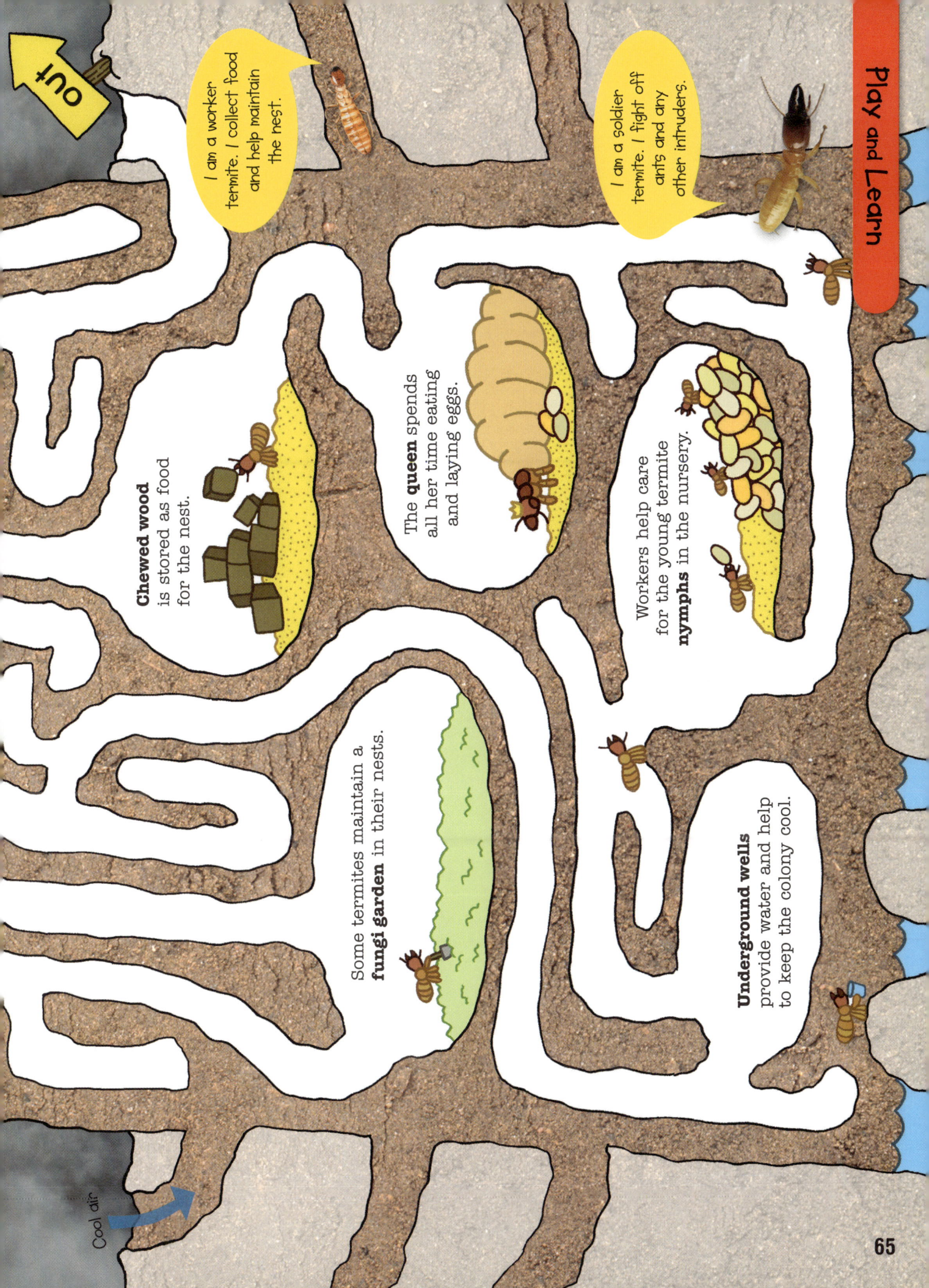

Busy bees

Honeybees might just be our best friends in the insect world. Not only do they pollinate more flowers than any other creature on Earth but they're also the reason we have delicious honey.

Facts about...

Pollination
As bees fly from plant to plant they spread pollen, which **helps the plants reproduce**. Other animals, such as birds and beetles, also pollinate—but not as much as bees.

How do bees make honey?
Bees don't make honey for us on purpose. It's actually a product of **nectar**, which is collected from flowers and turned into food for the entire colony.

COLOR in the flowers at the bottom to complete the scene.

Honeybee quiz

1. **What** do bees spread when they go from flower to flower?
2. **What** is honey a product of?
3. **What** are the three types of honeybees that live in a hive?
4. **Do** bumble bees gather nectar?
5. **How** many queens are there in a hive?

Facts about... Colonies

Bee colonies are very organized, and the bees work very hard. **Worker bees** tend to the queen, care for the young, collect and store nectar, and guard the hive.

Test Your Knowledge

ANSWER the questions in the honeybee quiz. Answers on pp. 92–93.

I gather nectar too, just not as much as honeybees do.

Bumblebee

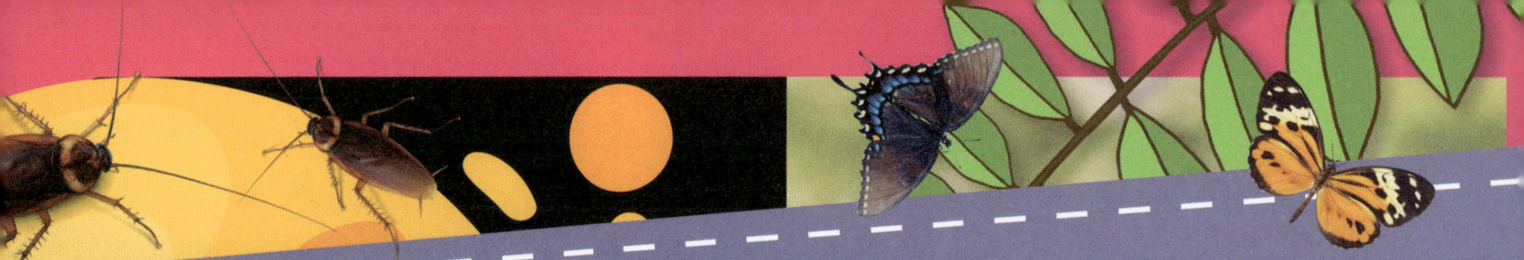

The unusual world of bugs

Insects and other arthropods are the most diverse creatures on Earth. This diversity means that many of them have very bizarre and extreme abilities.

1

2

3

4

5

6

FIND
where these pictures are on pp. 72–91. Check your answers on pp. 92–93.

Look and Find

Survival experts

Cockroaches are one of the toughest creatures on Earth and can survive in many extreme conditions. How extreme? You be the judge.

GUESS if each cockroach fact is true or false. Answers on pp. 92–93.

1 Even if a cockroach's head is cut off, it can survive for up to a week.

2 Cockroaches have existed for a billion years.

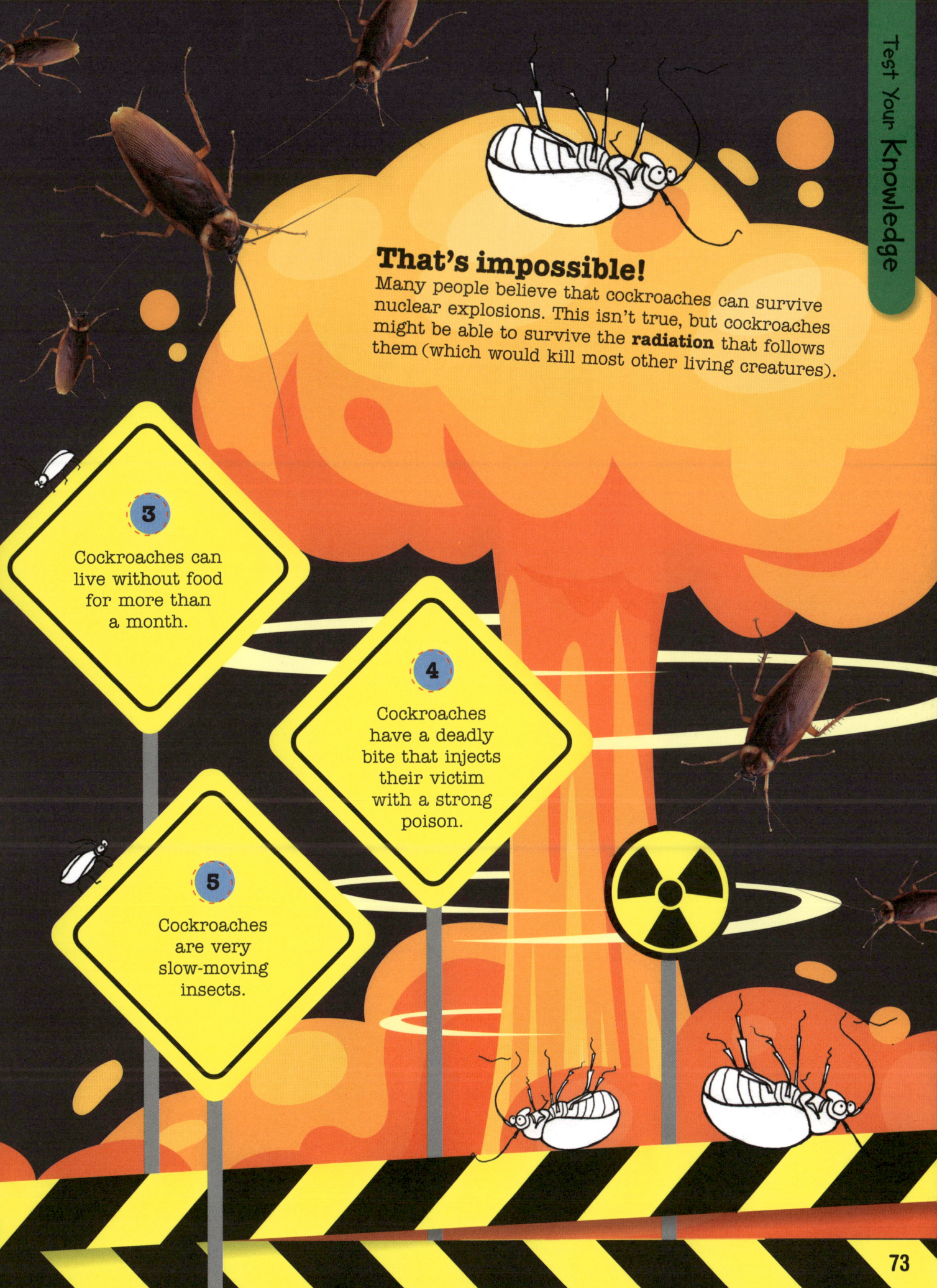

That's impossible!
Many people believe that cockroaches can survive nuclear explosions. This isn't true, but cockroaches might be able to survive the **radiation** that follows them (which would kill most other living creatures).

3 Cockroaches can live without food for more than a month.

4 Cockroaches have a deadly bite that injects their victim with a strong poison.

5 Cockroaches are very slow-moving insects.

Test Your Knowledge

WANTED
DEAD OR ALIVE

If you think the great white shark is the deadliest animal in the world, you're in for a surprise. Earth's most dangerous creature is actually the tiny mosquito!

Complete the picture

The world's deadliest animal

Why?
Mosquitoes don't have a deadly venom or a powerful sting, but they can carry and spread diseases such as malaria and yellow fever, which kill around **725,000 people each year**.

How?
Female mosquitoes suck human blood in order to gain the protein they need **to lay their eggs**. When they do this they can inject germs, which may spread and cause fatal diseases.

Test Your Knowledge

GUESS if each mosquito fact is true or false. Answers on pp. 92–93.

1 Mosquitoes have a deadly venom.

2 Mosquitoes can grow to be the size of tennis balls.

3 Mosquito saliva contains a painkiller so people can't feel their bites.

buzzzz buzzzzz buzzzzzzz

Actual size

Antenna

Proboscis

Wings

Many countries have wiped out the diseases spread by mosquitoes, but these diseases are still a big problem in poorer parts of the world.

4 Mosquito bites are very painful.

5 A mosquito's buzz is caused by its wings rubbing together.

6 Only female mosquitoes suck human blood.

Facts about... Malaria

The most common disease spread by mosquitoes is malaria. It causes a **strong fever**, which is very dangerous and can be fatal if it isn't treated.

75

Butterfly colors

Butterflies might be one of the prettiest types of insects, but their brightly colored patterns aren't just for show. They also help butterflies hide from, and even trick, predators.

COLOR each of the butterflies using the color key at the bottom right.

Light and dark
The female **eastern tiger swallowtail**, shown above and right, has two forms. One is bright yellow, the other is black.

Color each part as shown on the key.

Clever colors
Many, but not all, butterflies that are **orange-and-black** are poisonous, so predators often avoid any butterflies with that coloring.

I'm bright on top but when I close my wings it helps me hide.

Facts about... Symmetry

The patterns and colors on butterfly wings aren't just beautiful—they're also very interesting. Each wing looks like the **reflection** of the other. This is known as symmetry.

Read and Create

A clever disguise

When the peacock butterfly's wings are open it looks as if it has a **large pair of eyes** on its back. This can trick birds and other predators into thinking it's a much larger animal.

See if you can spot the "eyes" once the butterfly is colored in.

Key

1 2 3 4 5 6 7

Weird and wonderful

READ about the different kinds of arthropods in the world.

Red-kneed tarantula
Type: Arachnid
Top size: Up to 7 in (18 cm) long
Life span: Up to 30 years (females), up to 5 years (males)
Fact: It is sometimes kept as a pet. If a tarantula loses a leg, a new one can grow back in its place.

Queen fire ants can live for around 6 years.

Stick insect
Type: Insect
Top size: Up to 12 in (30 cm) long
Life span: Up to 2 years
Fact: This insect looks just like a twig, and sometimes plays dead to help keep itself safe from predators.

Fire ant
Type: Insect
Top size: Up to 0.2 in (6 mm) long
Life span: Up to 60 days
Fact: Fire ant colonies can contain more than 500,000 ants. Fire ants attack predators in large numbers in an organized way.

Tiger beetle
Type: Insect
Top size: Up to 1.5 in (4 cm) long
Life span: Up to 6 weeks
Fact: The Australian tiger beetle can move at speeds of up to 170 body lengths per second, which would be like a human running 217 mph (350 kph).

Decorator crab
Type: Crustacean
Top size: Up to 2 in (5 cm) long
Life span: Up to 10 years
Fact: This crab collects shells, seaweed, and other small animals, then attaches them to its body to help stay hidden.

Black widow spider
Type: Arachnid
Top size: Up to 1.5 in (4 cm) long
Life span: Up to 3 years
Fact: The female black widow has a red hourglass pattern on its abdomen, and its bite can deliver a deadly poison.

Firefly
Type: Insect
Top size: Up to 1 in (2.5 cm) long
Life span: Up to 1 month
Fact: Also known as a "lightning bug," a firefly is a type of beetle. It can emit a glowing light from special organs on its abdomen.

All of Earth's animals are amazing in one way or another, but no creatures come in as many strange forms as arthropods.

The puss moth caterpillar has a whiplike tail.

Some mayflies only live for a few minutes!

Armored millipede
Type: Myriapod
Top size: Up to 8 in (20 cm) long
Life span: Up to 10 years
Fact: In addition to its armor, this millipede has a poison to protect itself from predators.

Mayfly
Type: Insect
Top size: Up to 0.8 in (2 cm) long
Life span: Up to 2 days
Fact: An adult mayfly doesn't have a working mouth. It only lives long enough to reproduce, and doesn't need to eat.

Puss moth caterpillar
Type: Insect
Top size: Up to 3 in (7 cm) long
Life span: About 2 weeks (before becoming a puss moth)
Fact: This caterpillar waves around the whiplike section at its rear in defense. It can also spray acid at its enemies.

Read and Learn

A swarm of locusts

COUNT how many locusts there are in the scene. Answer on pp. 92–93.

These grasshoppers may not look like much, but after going through a dramatic change, they gather together in a feeding frenzy and cause huge damage to crops.

Don't count this timid green one!

Facts about...

Sudden change
Locusts can change from **timid green grasshoppers** into eating machines—becoming stronger, darker, and quicker, as well as changing their behavior.

We don't bite humans but we do like to eat their crops!

As locusts change they become organized, and eat any crops in sight.

Facts about... Getting bigger

Like a lot of other insects, as locusts grow they **shed their exoskeletons** and emerge looking different. This process is known as ecdysis.

Old skin

The locust wriggles out of its old skin, becoming larger and darker.

Look and find

Split personality

Locusts transform because of a chemical called **serotonin**. When food is in short supply and the hoppers gather in one place, their serotonin levels increase, which causes them to change.

TRUE OR FALSE? LARGE SWARMS SPREAD FOR MILES, AND CAN CONTAIN MORE THAN A BILLION LOCUSTS.

Yum! I'll eat everything in my path!

Silent hunters

The praying mantis is one of the deadliest hunters in the insect world. Its green color helps the insect blend into its environment, and it can rotate its head 180 degrees to look for nearby prey.

TRUE OR FALSE? THE PRAYING MANTIS IS A CLOSE RELATIVE OF THE COCKROACH.

A mantis will stay perfectly still until its prey is in reach.

1. Lunch

Spikes on its arms help it grip prey.

Suddenly, the mantis springs forward and snatches its prey.

2. Ahh!

Facts about... Mantis

After mating, the female praying mantis sometimes **bites off** the male's head. Scientists believe it does this to get extra energy to produce eggs.

We have something rare in insects called "binocular vision," which helps us spot prey.

Lying in wait

The praying mantis is an **ambush hunter**. It will hide in plain sight, staying motionless until its prey is nearby, then leap forward with lightning speed to snatch the victim.

The mantis brings its prey close and bites off its head!

Let me goooooo!

Crunch! Munch!

Quiz

1. What helps the praying mantis blend into its environment?

2. What kind of a hunter is the praying mantis?

3. How far can a praying mantis rotate its head?

4. What rare type of vision does the praying mantis have?

ANSWER the questions given in the quiz above. See answers on pp. 92–93.

Test Your Knowledge

17-year cicadas

Famous for having a very unusual life cycle, some cicadas spend up to 17 years underground—surfacing only to mate and enjoy a very short adult life.

COLOR the rest of the pictures to finish the cicada life cycles.

Fully grown cicadas have hard black bodies and amazing red eyes.

Facts about... Cicada songs

Millions of cicadas all buzzing together create a very distinct and unusual sound. It's actually the **loudest sound** in the insect world.

Some cicadas stay underground for 13 years.

For 17 years...

1 Young cicadas, also known as **nymphs**, can live underground for up to **17 years** feeding on the sap from tree roots.

4 Slowly their wings expand and their bodies harden and **turn black**. The cicadas then begin to look for a mate. To attract each other, the males make a buzzing noise and the females flick their wings together to make a clicking sound.

Read and Create

...one warm evening

2 When the time is right, **millions of cicadas** crawl out of the ground during the night and climb into trees.

The next day
Empty skin

3 The cicadas shed their skins and crawl out as adults. At first, they have shriveled wings and **soft white bodies**.

5 After mating the male dies instantly. The female then lays **hundreds of eggs** into gaps in the tree and dies shortly after.

A few months later...

6 Eventually the cicadas hatch from the eggs and the young cicadas fall to the ground. They then burrow underground to **wait for up to 17 years** to repeat the cycle.

Buzz! Buzz!

Some bugs can be very noisy. Many of them do this by rubbing parts of their bodies together. They use these sounds—which range from whining to chirruping—to communicate, find a mate, or scare away attackers.

FOLLOW the lines to find out the sound each of these bugs make.

Mosquito
A mosquito makes a loud whining sound. This noise is created by its wings, which flap about 400 times per second.

Wasp
When a wasp flies, its wings create a buzzing sound. This sound gets louder the faster its wings flap, which scares away enemies.

Facts about... Insect song

Many bugs use sounds to attract a mate. The male mole cricket digs a burrow entrance shaped like a trumpet, and sits at the bottom **making a churring sound**. The shape of the entrance allows the sound to reach as far as 1.2 miles (2 km).

Play and Learn

tap tap tap

Deathwatch beetle
This beetle taps its head on wood, creating a distinct sound of tapping to indicate its presence. It does this to attract a mate as well as to break down the wood for food.

hisssssssssss

Hissing cockroach
The Madagascar hissing cockroach pushes air out through breathing holes. This makes a hissing noise, which scares away attackers.

chirrup

Giant cicada
The male giant cicada is one of the loudest bugs. It has small drums, called tymbals, on its body, which make a high-pitched chirruping sound.

Helping bugs

Over the years, the insect population has been declining for many reasons. You'll need a counter and a dice to play this game. Then follow the path and read about how we can help insects survive.

Start

1

2 Recycling plastic helps keep it out of lakes, rivers, and seas. This protects aquatic invertebrates. **Roll again.**

12

13 Limit the use of pesticides because it not only kills pests but can also harm pollinators, such as bees. **Miss a turn.**

14

15

16 Deforestation can cause habitat loss, which makes it difficult for insects to survive. **Move back to step 14.**

17

18

19 Plant lots of flowers to provide a home for insects. Migratory insects can also enjoy a brief stopover. **Roll again.**

20

Design your own bug

The arthropod world is full of wonderful and fascinating creatures, and new species are being discovered all the time. Can you make up one of your own?

DRAW and color your own arthropod. You might want to add plants and create a home for it.

Draw and Learn

Answers

6–7
1. Page 21
2. Page 27
3. Page 25
4. Page 8–9
5. Page 18
6. Page 23
7. Page 14
8. Page 8
9. Page 17
10. Page 21
11. Page 24
12. Page 12

8–9
1. **True**
2. **True**
3. **True**
4. **False**. Their bodies have two or more parts.
5. **True**

10–11
1. About 2.5 ft (70 cm)
2. Millipede
3. About 310 million years ago
4. Decaying plants and insects

14–15
True or False?
True

16–17
1. 8 legs, Arachnid (spider)
2. 6 legs, Insect (honeybee)
3. 6 legs, Insect (beetle)
4. 6 legs, Insect (ladybird)
5. 10 legs, Crustacean (crab)
6. 8 legs, Arachnid (scorpion)
7. Around 60 legs, Myriapod (millipede)

18–19
1. **False**. There are millions of arthropod species in the world.
2. **True**
3. **False**. Some insects are harmful, not all.
4. **True**
5. **True**

20–21
True or False?
False. It is the largest butterfly.

24–25
1. c; 2. e; 3. a;
4. d; 5. b; 6. g; 7. f

28–29
1. Missing ant on the creeper
2. Size of the dragonfly
3. Different colored pot
4. Missing ladybug behind pot
5. Color of watering can
6. Size of snail
7. Missing earthworm from in front of the wheelbarrow
8. Color of daisy in the wheelbarrow

30–31
1. Page 50
2. Page 40
3. Page 42
4. Page 51
5. Page 40
6. Page 48
7. Page 37
8. Page 49
9. Page 43
10. Page 33
11. Page 36
12. Page 43

32–33
1. Forensic entomologist
2. Pest exterminator
3. Conservationist
4. Beekeeper
5. Entomologist

36–37
1. **True**
2. **False.** There are small flies but none that are totally invisible.
3. **False**. A human-sized cat flea could only jump about 1,115 ft (340 m) high.
4. **False**. A moth can fly up to 30 mph (48 kph).
5. **True**
6. **True**

40–41
1. Harmful (aphids)
2. Helpful & harmful (fruit flies)
3. Harmful (fleas)
4. Helpful & harmful (bees)
5. Helpful (dung beetle)
6. Helpful & harmful (maggots)
7. Helpful & harmful (termites)
8. Harmful (mosquitoes)

42–43
True or False?
False. Scavengers eat rotting

plants, dead bodies of other animals, garbage, and even our food.

44–45
1. To hide from predators or to surprise their prey
2. Forest leaf grasshopper
3. Treehoppers
4. Cracker butterfly

46–47
Waterbug: 6
Scorpion: 2
Silkworm pupae: 12
Shrimp: 5
Mealworms: 15
Crickets: 3
True or False?
True

50–51
1. c
2. b
3. d
4. a

52–53
1. Page 66
2. Page 60
3. Page 63
4. Page 58
5. Page 57
6. Page 58
7. Page 59
8. Page 67
9. Page 67
10. Page 55
11. Page 65
12. Page 58

56–57
1. **False**. Ants have been around for about 140–168 million years.
2. **True**

3. **True**
4. **False**. The Japanese Carpenter Ant can grow up to be 17 mm (0.7 in).
5. **True**
6. **True**

58–59
1. b. Pincers
2. a. Five times stronger than a piece of steel
3. c. Mites and ticks
4. a. In their webs

62–63
True or False?
True

64–65
True or False?
True

66–67
1. Pollen
2. Nectar
3. The queen, the workers, and the drones
4. Yes
5. One queen

70–71
1. Page 73
2. Page 77
3. Page 86
4. Page 79
5. Page 85
6. Page 91
7. Page 85
8. Page 83
9. Page 79
10. Page 74
11. Page 84
12. Page 81

72–73
1. **True** (but they will eventually starve)
2. **False**. They have been around for more than 300 million years.
3. **True** (but they won't survive for long without water)
4. **False**. Their bite is not deadly, but can cause an allergic reaction.
5. **False**. They can move swiftly.

74–75
1. **False**. They are not venomous.
2. **False**. The largest mosquito can be about 1.6 in (4 cm).
3. **True**
4. **False**. Mosquito bites are not very painful.
5. **True**
6. **True**

80–81
33 locusts
True or False?
True

82–83
1. Its green color
2. Ambush hunter
3. 180 degrees
4. Binocular vision
True or False?
True

Glossary

abdomen
Rear section of an insect's body

aggressive
Behaving angrily, with a willingness to attack others

ambush
To attack something by surprise from a hidden place

ancestor
Relative who lived a long time ago

antennae
Pair of sense organs, also called feelers, located near the front of an insect's head

barbed
Something that has clusters of short spikes

bioluminescent
Ability to produce light within the body

breed
When an animal mates and creates a baby

burrow
Hole or tunnel dug in the ground by an animal for it to live in

chrysalis
Hard casing a butterfly wraps itself in during metamorphosis

colony
Group of insects that live together

conserve
To save or protect something

decay
To rot, decompose, or break down

deciduous forest
Forest with trees that lose their leaves in winter

deforestation
Cutting down trees and destroying forests

descendant
Animal in later generations of their ancestors

disguise
Altering appearance to avoid being recognized

diverse
Group containing a wide variety of things, people, or animals

ecosystem
Living community of plants and animals found together in their environment

evolve
The way living things change and adapt over time to help them survive

eyespot
Eyelike marking on an insect

exoskeleton
Hard outer casing of animals, such as arthropods, that do not have an internal skeleton

fossil
Remains of a dead animal or plant, which has been preserved in rock over time

frenzy
Extreme excitement or wild behavior

habitat
Natural home of an animal or plant

infest
When insects, such as termites or ants, are present in large numbers and cause damage to plants or homes

mandibles
Two parts of an insect's mouth that are used to grab food or prey

mate
When a male and female animal produce young

metamorphosis
Process by which some young insects transform into a different form when they reach adulthood

migratory
Describes animals that travel from one place to another, usually when the seasons change

nectar
Sweet liquid made by some flowers

paralyze
To cause an animal to lose the ability to move or feel sensation in its body

pesticide
Chemical that farmers use to control pests that harm plants

pincers
A pair of large, clawlike body parts used by an arthropod for feeding or defense

poisonous
Something that causes harm if eaten or touched

pollinate
Taking pollen from one plant to another to produce new plant seeds

predator
Animal that hunts other animals for food

prehistoric
Ancient time before recorded history

prey
Animal that is hunted by another animal for food

segmented
Divided into different parts

slender
Something thin and delicate

swarm
Large group of flying insects

translucent
Something that allows light to pass through it

unsanitary
Something dirty and unhealthy that might cause diseases

venomous
Able to produce venom (poison) and inject it by means of stings or bites

Acknowledgments

Original edition: Design Clare Shedden, Sadie Thomas, Samantha Richiardi, Charlotte Bull, Stefan Georgiou; **Editorial** James Mitchem; **Illustration** Chris Howker, Jake McDonald.

DORLING KINDERSLEY would like to thank: Roohi Sehgal for editorial support, Rushil Pradhan for design support on the jacket, and Phil Hunt for proofreading.

The publisher would like to thank the following for their kind permission to reproduce their photographs:

(Key: a-above; b-below/bottom; c-center; f-far; l-left; r-right; t-top)

1 Dreamstime.com: Kruglovorda (cb). **3 123RF.com:** Tim Hester / timhester (tl). **Dreamstime.com:** Andreykuzmin (tc/dirt); Filmfoto (tc). **4 Alamy Stock Photo:** Redmond Durrell (cra). **Dreamstime.com:** Benchart (cb); Robyn Mackenzie / Robynmac (ca). **6 Dreamstime.com:** Grafner (clb/background); Marcouliana (crb); Slowmotiongli (clb); THPStock (br). **7 Alamy Stock Photo:** Redmond Durrell (clb). **Dreamstime.com:** Aleksandra Nazarova (br/background); Photka (tr). **8-9 Dreamstime.com:** Andreykuzmin (dirt); Photka (leaves); Marcouliana (c). **10 Alamy Stock Photo:** Natural History Museum, London (ca); Wide Eye Pictures (bl). **Dreamstime.com:** Digitalimagined (ca/x2). **10-11 Dreamstime.com:** Anankkml (Centipede x 3); Tartilastock (cactus); Joseph Calev (centipede x 2). **11 Alamy Stock Photo:** Sabena Jane Blackbird (ca). **Dreamstime.com:** Ambassador806 (br). **Science Photo Library:** Gilles Mermet (cl). **12 Dreamstime.com:** Aleksandra Nazarova (3xwhite background). **13 Dreamstime.com:** Maxkrasnov (c). **14 Dorling Kindersley:** Colin Keates / Natural History Museum, London (ca/dragonfly). **Dreamstime.com:** Isselee (crb/Diadem spider). **Fotolia:** Eric Isselee (tc/stick insect). **16-17 Dreamstime.com:** Les Cunliffe (torn paper); Smileus (frame). **Getty Images:** Photodisc / Dieter Spears. **16 Dreamstime.com:** Isselee (cra). **17 Alamy Stock Photo:** Redmond Durrell (bl). **Dorling Kindersley:** Colin Keates / Natural History Museum, London (cla, cr). **18 Dreamstime.com:** Christophe Testi (tr). **18-19 Dreamstime.com:** Les Cunliffe (5xTorn paper); Sataporn Jiwjalaen / Onairjiw (background). **19 Dorling Kindersley:** Colin Keates / Natural History Museum, London (br). **20 Dorling Kindersley:** Frank Greenaway / Natural History Museum, London (clb); Colin Keates / Natural History Museum, London (cr). **Dreamstime.com:** Alinamd. **Shutterstock.com:** Maria Shipakina (tr); Cheng Wei (ca). **21 Alamy Stock Photo:** Nature Picture Library / Alex Hyde (crb). **Dorling Kindersley:** Frank Greenaway / Natural History Museum, London (tl, tr, c, cb, cra, crb/Tiger Moth). **22-23 Dorling Kindersley:** Stephen Oliver (ca). **Dreamstime.com:** Filindmitriy86 (cb/pebbles). **22 Dreamstime.com:** Anankkml (br). **23 Dreamstime.com:** THPStock (bl). **24-25 Dreamstime.com:** Grafner. **25 Alamy Stock Photo:** Sabena Jane Blackbird (bc); Nature Photographers Ltd / Paul R. Sterry (crb). **Dreamstime.com:** Glenn Price (cb); Slowmotiongli (clb). **27 Alamy Stock Photo:** David J Slater (clb). **Dreamstime.com:** Spineback (tl). **Science Photo Library:** Dant Fenolio (clb/Motyxia). **29 Dreamstime.com:** Fotofred (cla). **Getty Images / iStock:** Antagain (ca). **30 Dreamstime.com:** Elena Elisseeva (clb/Daisy); Vitalche (tl); Pavel Trankov (clb/Wasp); Samuel Micut (clb); Luayana (br/bug, br/leaves). **Getty Images / iStock:** gyro (br). **Getty Images:** Moment Open / Adegsm (cl). **31 Dreamstime.com:** Palex66 (cl); Vaeenma (br). **Getty Images / iStock:** gyro (tr/background). **32 Alamy Stock Photo:** Alfred Schauhuber / Imagebroker (cra). **34 Dorling Kindersley:** Frank Greenaway / Natural History Museum, London (br). **Getty Images / iStock:** E+ / traveler1116 (tl). **35 Dreamstime.com:** Roman Charushin (cla); Digitalimagined (ca); Sergey Galushko (clb). **Getty Images / iStock:** E+ / traveler1116 (cra). **Shutterstock.com:** I Wayan Sumatika (cr). **36 Dorling Kindersley:** The Tank Museum, Bovington (crb). **Dreamstime.com:** Boonchuay Iamsumang (cb). **37 Dreamstime.com:** Weerapat Kiatdumrong (c). **40 Dorling Kindersley:** Alan Buckingham (tl). **40-41 Dreamstime.com:** Benchart (Mosquito x 5). **41 Dreamstime.com:** Banorsolic (cla/cb); Yurix (tl); Duncan Noakes (tr). **42 Dreamstime.com:** Antonel (crb/flower); Pavel Trankov (clb); Samuel Micut (clb/crb); Elena Elisseeva (clb/Daisies); Pasqueflower (cb); Katrina Brown (c); Valentina Razumova (cb/worm). **43 Dreamstime.com:** Maksym Bondarchuk (br); Le Thuy Do (tr); Kruglovorda (cra); Palex66 (cla); Eduardo Gonzalez Diaz (cb); Julia Sudnitskaya (crb); Pasqueflower (cb/grass); Vaeenma (bc); Matthijs Kuijpers (clb). **44 Dorling Kindersley:** Thomas Marent (cla, cl, cr). **45 Dreamstime.com:** Sandra Standbridge (cr). **46-47 Alamy Stock Photo:** MiscellaneouStock (silkworm). **Getty Images / iStock:** ISvyatkovsky (spoon x 2). **47 Dreamstime.com:** Johnbell (cb/Scorpion x 2); Dmytro Synelnychenko (r/texture). **48 Dreamstime.com:** Luayana (cla, cl). **Getty Images / iStock:** DigitalVision Vectors / kathykonkle (bl). **48-49 Getty Images / iStock:** gyro (b, t). **49 Dreamstime.com:** Luayana (tr). **50 Dreamstime.com:** Vitalche (cl). **Getty Images:** Moment Open / Adegsm (br). **51 Depositphotos Inc:** DesignPicsInc (bl). **Dreamstime.com:** Olgakotsareva (tl/background). **52 Depositphotos Inc:** Ale-ks (bl). **Dorling Kindersley:** Thomas Marent (crb). **Dreamstime.com:** Puripatch Lokakalin (tl); Okea (cra/tarantula). **Shutterstock.com:** Michal Sloviak (cra). **53 Corbis:** Bloomimage (tr). **Dorling Kindersley:** Dave King / Science Museum, London (crb/candle). **Dreamstime.com:** Iquacu (crb). **Shutterstock.com:** ChristopherRM (br). **54 Dorling Kindersley:** Colin Keates / Natural History Museum (ca). **55 Dorling Kindersley:** Dave King / Science Museum, London (c/candle). **Dreamstime.com:** Iquacu (c/Honey); Wd2007 (bc). **Fotolia:** Auris (ca). **56 Depositphotos Inc:** Ale-ks (crb/bl). **Dreamstime.com:** Henrikhl (cb/br). **57 Depositphotos Inc:** Ale-ks (bl/br). **Dorling Kindersley:** Thomas Marent. **Dreamstime.com:** Henrikhl (cb/bc). **58 Dorling Kindersley:** Thomas Marent (cl, cr). **Dreamstime.com:** Isselee (clb). **Shutterstock.com:** ChristopherRM (tl). **59 Dreamstime.com:** Matthijs Kuijpers (cla). **60 Alamy Stock Photo:** blickwinkel / B. Trapp (bl). **Dreamstime.com:** Miroslaw Kijewski (cr); Okea (tc); Andrei Moldovan (ca/crb). **Shutterstock.com:** Michal Sloviak (cla). **63 Alamy Stock Photo:** Redmond Durrell (bc/ladybird); Nature Picture Library / Chris Mattison (cb/jewel beetle); Brian Hagiwara (br). **Dorling Kindersley:** Gyuri Csoka Cyorgy (bc); Colin Keates / Natural History Museum, London (ca); Colin Keates / Natural History Museum (cb). **Getty Images / iStock:** imv (tc). **64-65 Dreamstime.com:** Photomo. **66 Dreamstime.com:** Puripatch Lokakalin (tr). **66-67 Corbis:** Bloomimage. **70 Dorling Kindersley:** Thomas Marent (crb). **Dreamstime.com:** Filmfoto (br/Green leaf); Janice Mccafferty (tc); Sergei Razvodovskij (br); Oakdalecat (cr). **71 Depositphotos Inc:** YAYImages (tr). **Dreamstime.com:** Patrick W Barry (cl). **74 Fotolia:** Vadim Yerofeyev. **75 Dreamstime.com:** Elena Andreeva (cr); Sergeyoch (cra). **Getty Images / iStock:** nechaev-kon (br). **76 Dreamstime.com:** Janice Mccafferty (ca). **78 Fotolia:** Eric Isselee (cla). **Getty Images / iStock:** E+ / Stephanie Phillips (cb). **79 Dorling Kindersley:** Frank Greenaway / Natural History Museum, London (ca); Thomas Marent (b). **80-81 123RF.com:** Vassiliy Prikhodko. **82-83 Dreamstime.com:** Patrick W Barry; Maldesowhat (tc). **84-85 Depositphotos Inc:** YAYImages. **86 Alamy Stock Photo:** WILDLIFE GmbH (cl). **Dreamstime.com:** Isselee (bl); Oakdalecat (cra). **87 Dreamstime.com:** David Carillet (cra); Piman Khrutmuang (tl). **88 Dreamstime.com:** Aputin308 (cla); Pinkpueblo (tc/ca); Clare Jackson (bc); Pasqueflower (bc/grass). **88-89 Dreamstime.com:** Victoria Shibut (t). **89 Dreamstime.com:** Elena Elisseeva (c); Pinkpueblo (br); Henrikhl (cb). **Shutterstock.com:** Michal Sloviak (cb). **90 123RF.com:** Tim Hester / timhester (tc). **Dorling Kindersley:** Colin Keates / Natural History Museum, London (cl). **Dreamstime.com:** Sergei Razvodovskij (cl/Leaf). **90-91 Dreamstime.com:** Filmfoto (tc/bc). **Getty Images:** Photodisc / Harvey Tsoi. **91 Dreamstime.com:** Fotofermer (crb); Christophe Testi (cr); Sergei Razvodovskij (bc). **92 Dreamstime.com:** Andrei Moldovan (tc); Okea (cra). **93 Dreamstime.com:** Luayana (crb); Vitalche (bc). **94 Getty Images / iStock:** E+ / traveler1116 (tr). **95 Dorling Kindersley:** Gyuri Csoka Cyorgy (crb). **Dreamstime.com:** Andreykuzmin (br); Roman Charushin (tr)

Cover images: *Front:* **123RF.com:** Tim Hester / timhester cb; **Dorling Kindersley:** Colin Keates / Natural History Museum cra, Colin Keates / Natural History Museum, London bc; **Dreamstime.com:** Roman Charushin crb, Fotofermer crb/ (leaf), Johnbell cl, Marcouliana clb, br, Thawats tr; *Back:* **Dorling Kindersley:** Gyuri Csoka Cyorgy crb; **Dreamstime.com:** Boonchuay Iamsumang clb, Isselee tl; *Spine:* **Dorling Kindersley:** Gyuri Csoka Cyorgy cb, Colin Keates / Natural History Museum, London ca

All other images © Dorling Kindersley Limited